Overcoming Suicidal Thoughts:

A Guide for Transforming Struggle into Strength

by

Stanislaus Klaus

Contents

Introduction

Most people see themselves in a certain way and believe that they have nothing to do with the subject of suicide. This is absolutely not true because everyone is involved and everyone can be suicidal at one point or another. Even if you are not directly affected, then someone close to you may be affected. For this reason, it is necessary to equip oneself with the right information and the necessary knowledge to be able to cope with the condition of being suicidal.

The interesting and maybe shocking thing in the stories of people who eventually committed suicide is that it just seems like a flash. The pressure is so much that they do not usually have the time to fight the thought or to think it through. This means it is usually spontaneous. A certain man who survived a suicide jump from a bridge explains how his heart was filled with instant regret as he jumped of the lagoon. He realized instantly that this was not what he wanted. He really wanted to live.

This is the same case with several people who committed suicide. Once the trigger comes, it is so strong that it blocks out every other thing and tries to push the individuals into thinking that what they really want is to be away from this world. Understanding this and many other details related to suicide could be helpful when dealing with suicidal thoughts yourself or while dealing with people in such situations.

The main point that you should note is that suicidal thoughts can be overcome. The first step is to get the requisite knowledge which is what you have in your hands right now. It is about overcoming emotions and accepting negativity as a part of life. There is no one in the world who is only seeing the positive part of life. In fact, for every bad situation you may face, there is someone out there who has faced worse. This will help you understand that it is not just about what happens to you but how you respond to the things that happen to you.

The topic being discussed has a lot to do with despair. So many people give in to despair and that is the beginning of their tuning into suicidal thoughts. When you get to the point when you no longer have the hope in the future, you fall into despair and feel that there is no need to keep on living. This is the struggle that goes on within and hardly noticed by anyone on the outside. However, there is always a way to transform these moments of struggle into strength. It begins with awareness. It begins with the realization of the trick being played by circumstances. Illusions trying to assume the position of reality. This is where the first step of knowledge gaining comes in. This is the ideal means through which all the clouds of despair and confusion will be dispersed.

Stanislaus Klaus

What is Suicide?

The World Health Organization (WHO) defines suicide as "the deliberate act of taking one's own life." This definition highlights the fact that it is a deliberate and this implies a decision made by the individual to end things, believing that this is the best decision at that moment. The National Institute of Mental Health (NIMH) defines suicide as "a tragic event that occurs when a person takes their own lives." The highlight there is the word "tragic."

This means that suicide is not a positive thing both to the individual and to the society. It is tragic in the sense that it neither brings joy to the society nor satisfaction to the individual. Often, in the cases of a successful suicide, the friends and neighbours feel downcast and so to say ashamed. They feel that they have let a fellow down by not being there for him or for her.

The word suicide is a coinage from two Latin words 'sui' – oneself and 'cidere' – to strike down/ to kill. Suicide is the deliberate killing of oneself. The word deliberate is important in the definition of Suicide because a person can kill himself without intending to do so. In that case it is not suicide. Suicide involves a conscious act of making plans to end one's own life and it is usually voluntary.

Whether a person is being acted upon by an external force or not, if a person eventually kills himself, it is suicide. There are cases where several people who attended a lecture by a particular philosopher named Hegesias killed themselves thereafter. He was known as the death persuader and was banned in several cities from delivering any public lectures. His book Death by Starvation was also banned and did not survive except in commentaries in other works.

Some key aspects of suicide include:

- Intentionality: The person intends to end their life.

- Voluntary action: The person takes deliberate steps to carry out the act.

- Self-inflicted: The harm is inflicted by the person themselves.

Despite these factors which point directly to the individual, we still see the bearing in the society and how it affects many other people apart from the victim.

Causes of Suicide

There are several causes of suicide but all usually begin with depression. It usually follows a pattern, although not defined, but recognizable. Suicide usually begins with a trigger which leads to depression, suicidal thoughts and eventually depression. One or more of these below may be the cause of suicide:

#1 Feeling like a burden on family and society

Some people fall into extreme depressive thoughts that make them feel like they are a burden on other persons in society. This is usually the case when one is afflicted with one severe illness or another or bedridden for a long while. These persons are unable to help themselves and depend on the help of other people to eat, bath etc. They may feel like they are doing something good for the society by taking their own lives and liberating those saddled with the responsibility of taking care of them.

This points to the ability not just to give help but to receive help. Some people have not developed the ability to let other people help them. As such, at the critical moments of their lives when they just need to allow other people help them live through, they may try to run away from such scenario by ending their own lives. This is not a positive thing because most of those who are taking up the task of watching over them are doing so wholeheartedly out of love.

#2 Life disasters

Life disasters include events that tend to shatter one's life which has taken a relatively long time to build. This can include the loss of one's building or other properties, loss of a job or an investment, loss of a loved one, broken relationships etc. These situations can lead one into depression and eventually into suicide. What is considered at the time of figuring out whatever the disaster is that has befallen one is usually the length of time or amount of energy put into building what has been shattered by the disaster. Most times, the judgment of whether or whether not an event can lead one to commit suicide is dependent on the weight the event has from the perspective of the concerned individual.

Apart from natural disasters, there are other events that can affect a whole group entirely. A pandemic just like the COVID-19 can displace an economy and affect individuals in a number of ways. It is true that there is a general ideology of the effects that pandemics, natural disasters and wars can come with, however, every individual's situation is unique and some people feel the heat more than others. Therefore, it can be the cause of suicidal thoughts for one who is weighed down by these occurrences.

#3 Mental health issues

Some of the mental issues come along with hallucinations that may trigger the mind to have a different view of the world. In this situation, the individual is trapped inside the world created by hallucinations and he begins to act as though being controlled by forces beyond him. Sometimes, the manner of speech shows that there is a different activity going on in his mental state and which he believes as real. This can get to the point where the world is despised and all efforts from the patient will be to embrace the world in his head through suicide.

Those who have mental health patients are prone to commit suicide because their mental states are already affected. They seem to have a greater chance of slipping into suicidal thoughts because they interact less with the physical world and want to leave it as soon as they can. Sometimes, the mental issues make them feel insecure amidst other people. They cannot stay calmly around others because they feel threatened by their presence. Within a space of time, they begin to doubt that they are meant to be in this world and finally may end up killing themselves to get free from world and all its troubles.

#4 Financial Crisis

When people begin to get so much responsibilities especially in the area of finance, they begin to seek ways to solve them by making money. However, when these means prove abortive, then comes to flight instinct and the individual suddenly wants to run away from all his responsibilities forever. This is when suicide will be considered as a way of putting an end to endless struggles to manage financial responsibilities.

An example of this situation is a family man with children who gets fired from his job. He does not have enough savings and is unable to get a job within the next few months. Sooner or later, the responsibilities of household rent, children's school fees and other maintenance fees will begin to engulf him. Depending on his mental strength, he may end up taking his own life as a way of running away from the shame of not being able to fulfil responsibilities and the struggle of being unsuccessful in his efforts.

#5 Societal Pressure and Shame

For some reasons, sometimes the pressure in society tends to be directed to a few individuals and attention is given to them, monitoring and judging their every move. On the other hand, individuals can feel that the society is putting pressure on them even if it is not true. This puts these individuals out of their nature as they have to act cautiously all the time to avoid criticism from people. Sometimes, the pressure is out of xenophobic tendencies or racial characteristics. In this case, certain people are stigmatized and treated awkwardly in society. As a result, these people stay reserved and have to put in twice the work in order to survive in society.

Shame can also lead to suicide because each person has a boundary of shame. When someone does an act which he considers as shameful, he may have the thoughts to kill himself. Also, when an individual's boundary of shame is crossed and the person is abused in one way or the other, there is a tendency to also tilt towards suicide. It is relative in every individual as some have a stronger mental capacity to endure than other people while others have less.

What does it mean to be suicidal or who is a suicidal person?

A suicidal person is one who is undergoing grave depression and is considering to end his or her own life. A suicidal person is in a suicide crisis and at the verge of ending life. These are shown through suicidal symptoms that will be listed below. Before one becomes suicidal, depression must have taken place and a prolonged depression is then the result of being suicidal.

Symptoms of a Suicidal Person

The symptoms of suicide can already be traced from the symptoms of depression since it is depression that eventually leads to suicidal thoughts. These symptoms can be classified under various categories like verbal cues, physical signs, emotional signs, behavioural changes and other red flags. Below are some of the common symptoms associated with suicide:

#1 Shuts off social communication and spends more time alone.

Shutting off social communication and spending more time alone can be a concerning sign that someone may be struggling with suicidal thoughts or mental health issues. Social withdrawal can amplify negative thoughts and feelings, reduce support networks and coping mechanisms, increase feelings of isolation and loneliness, and make it harder to seek help.

If you notice someone avoiding phone calls, texts, or meetings, canceling plans or appointments, refusing to engage in conversations, or spending excessive time alone or in isolation, reach out and express concern. Encourage open conversation, offer support and company, and help connect them with mental health resources. Remember, withdrawal can be a coping mechanism, but it can also worsen mental health. By recognizing the signs and offering support, you can help someone reconnect and find the help they need.

#2 Appears sad and gloomy most of the time.

A person struggling with suicidal thoughts may exhibit persistent sadness and gloominess, which can be noticeable in their demeanor, behavior, and interactions. They may appear withdrawn, lethargic, and disconnected from others, displaying a lack of interest in activities they once enjoyed. This persistent sadness can manifest physically, such as through slumped posture, tearfulness, or changes in appetite or sleep patterns. Their speech may also become monotone, hesitant, or lacking in enthusiasm, conveying a sense of hopelessness and despair.

#3 Speaks about the other side (heaven, hell or the spiritual realm)

A person struggling with suicidal thoughts may exhibit an unusual preoccupation with the afterlife, frequently discussing heaven, hell, or the spiritual realm. They may express a fascination with the concept of an afterlife, seeking reassurance about what lies beyond or wondering if there's more to life than their current struggles. This fixation can be a coping mechanism, providing an escape from their emotional pain or a sense of control over their circumstances. However, it can also indicate a growing detachment from the present life, signaling a potential risk of suicidal behavior.

#4 Speaks about death and the feeling of death

A person struggling with suicidal thoughts may frequently speak about death, exhibiting a morbid fascination with the concept, and may directly express a desire to die, talk about death as a solution to their problems, or romanticize it as a release. They may ask about the nature of death, make macabre jokes, or discuss their own funeral. This preoccupation can stem from feelings of hopelessness, emotional pain, isolation, and loss of purpose. If you notice these conversational cues, listen attentively and empathetically, avoid dismissing their concerns, and encourage professional help.

#5 Acts awkwardly as though existing on another plane

A person struggling with suicidal thoughts may exhibit an unsettling detachment from reality, acting as though they exist on another plane. Their behavior may seem distant, disconnected, or surreal, manifesting in awkward interactions, delayed responses, or staring blankly into space. They may appear disconnected from their surroundings, display flat emotions, or show an unnatural calmness, indicating a growing separation from the world around them. This dissociation can be a coping mechanism, providing temporary escape from overwhelming emotional pain. However, it's crucial to recognize this behavior as a potential warning sign and approach the individual with empathy and concern, encouraging open conversation and professional help to prevent further disconnection and potential harm.

#6 Writes dark poems and essays

Creating dark, introspective, and potentially disturbing written content can be a warning sign of suicidal thoughts. Individuals struggling with suicidal ideation may express their emotional turmoil through creative outlets like poetry, essays, or journaling. Their writing may feature recurring themes of death, despair, hopelessness, or existential crises, potentially including graphic or disturbing imagery. While creative expression can be therapeutic, pay attention if their work: intensifies in darkness or frequency, displays fixation on mortality, or explicitly mentions suicidal intentions. Encourage open conversation, empathy, and professional help, recognizing that their writing may be a cry for support.

#7 Speaks in a dark manner even in the common situations

A person struggling with suicidal thoughts may consistently express dark, pessimistic, or morbid views, even in everyday conversations. They might inject bleak humor, morbid references, or hopeless sentiments into casual discussions, making others uncomfortable. This persistent darkness can be a red flag, revealing underlying emotional pain. Listen for phrases that suggest: hopelessness ("What's the point?"), despair ("I'll never escape this"), or fascination with death ("I wonder what it's like to die"). Such language may indicate a cry for help.

#8 Talks so much about how much people cannot understand what he or she is passing through.

person struggling with suicidal thoughts may repeatedly express feelings of being misunderstood, isolated, and disconnected from others. They may lament that no one truly comprehends their emotional pain, saying phrases like "You wouldn't understand," "You can't relate," or "I'm completely alone in this." This sense of disconnection can exacerbate feelings of hopelessness and despair. Listen attentively if they express a feeling invisible or ignored, being trapped in their own world, difficulty articulating emotions, frustration with others' lack of empathy.

5 Important Tips for Suicide Prevention: What you must know

There may not be laid down rules about suicide prevention but from the causes of suicide, we can decipher what things we can do in order to prevent it. The tips for suicide prevention are some of the things one can undertake in day-to-day activities in order to reduce the chances of becoming suicidal. There are two sides to suicide prevention tips. One is in relation to the one who is feeling suicidal and the second is in relation to the person who is close to one who is suicidal. Both the individual who is feeling suicidal and the one close to a suicidal person have roles to play.

Suicide prevention refers to the steps that individuals or groups can take in order to decrease the rate of suicide cases and the chances of being suicidal. It could be seen as a series of efforts to reduce the risk of suicide. This involves strategies that can aid in preventing suicide. Suicide prevention is possible at all levels; the individual, the family, the society etc.

When put into consideration, the tips below can be a great way to push depression and suicide far away from yourself. It is necessary to understand that there is a process that leads to depression and suicidal thoughts. If these can be recognized and avoided, then there are greater chances of preventing suicide.

#1 Build social and emotional intelligence

Intelligence in social and emotional life is paramount to the development of a healthy mindset and personality. Disbalance in any of these areas will eventually lead to a reduction of self-esteem, depression and eventually suicide. Social intelligence has to do with mastery of the associations we find ourselves in and control of the people we let into our lives and the effects they have in our lives. Man is a social being and must interact with other people. If he is to live properly, he must learn how to exercise his social qualities and how to accept other people and their concerns too.

Emotional intelligence has to do with an upgraded understanding of oneself that leads to acting consciously out of reasoning rather than reacting to situations without restraint. Emotional intelligence demands maturity from the individual in accepting responsibility, not denying feelings that are obviously present and facing reality as it is without wishful thinking or fantasizing. Both social intelligence and emotional intelligence will help the individual develop the capacity to repel suicidal thoughts and see meaning in life. Some people who want to commit suicide are doing it simply because they wish to run away from their conceived responsibilities. However, with social and emotional intelligence, this will no longer be the case.

#2 Do not bottle up yourself

Bottling up yourself in this situation entails revealing top personal secrets to other people who could use them against you. Most people tend to easily give out some of their secret information to other people once they feel that the other party can be trusted.

However, when a problem arises in the relationship, the secrets have already been divulged and can be used against them. This keeps them uncomfortable and continuously in thought because they know that they have bottled themselves up.

It is better not to divulge whatever you consider a top-secret that could ruin your life when revealed. In this way, you are safe from all the possible occurrences that would take place if your secret is divulged. Most importantly, you enjoy peace of mind because you are not afraid that someone somewhere may be leaking your secret. Such thoughts continue to keep you insecure and will lead to suicidal thoughts when there is a problem between you and the person you consider your secret bearer.

#3 Reflect on positive aspects of life

One of the reasons that people become suicidal is because they focus on the negatives in their lives and forget the positives. This makes one see everything in life as sorrowful and not worth it. However, when you make it a priority to recount positive aspects of your life regularly, you will have a greater chance of preventing suicidal thoughts. One of the best ways to apply this is by putting it down into writing. You can take a jotter and write down the good things that have occurred in your life within the past few days, weeks, months or years.

Take the time to remember as much as you can and explain the details of each of the good things you consider as a blessing. Since writing is a psycho-neuro-motor activity, it will influence your thought pattern and make you see the light at the end of the tunnel. It is only with such positive practices as this that you will begin to see the light at the end of the tunnel even in difficult moments.

#4 Remember your place in society

Sometimes, people feel suicidal because they forget their place in society or they have a distorted view of their place in society. In order to avoid suicide and any form of depression, it is necessary to always call to mind your place in society. Everyone has a place in society. Starting from your position in the family, your place in school, your workplace, friendship circle etc. All these are places of relevance and whether you like it or not you have responsibilities towards others in these areas in as much as people have responsibilities towards you.

In the same way, your presence is an advantage to others because you share burdens together and help each other feel happy and productive. These are some of the things that are forgotten at the point of deciding to commit suicide. If you are able to remind yourself of your relevance to other people in society, then you will not think of yourself as useless and in return, you will prevent suicide and suicidal thoughts.

#5 Overcome depression without medication

Some people think that it is right to look for whatever means possible to deal with feelings of depression and lack of motivation. This is not true because over time it will become addictive and lead to worse stages of depression that will induce suicidal thoughts. It is important that you should learn how to overcome depression without medication so that you can begin to trust yourself and not trust drugs that are harmful to your immune system.

It is true that there are so many antidepressants available at different places but their availability does not mean we should use them as we like. The first thing is to recognize that your problems are beyond those temporary reliefs given by those medications. The short-term gratification and secretion of hormones like dopamine and serotonin do not guarantee a cessation of your problems. Medication in the treatment of depression is not a primary solution but a secondary one that is used side by side with counselling and other methods that thrive to heal from the roots.

Final Words

As you come to the end of this book, remember that you are not alone. Your struggle, though unique, is shared by many, and most importantly, your strength, resilience, and courage are greater than your darkest moments.

Suicide may have once seemed like an escape, but now you know it's not the answer. You've learned to confront the shadows, to seek help, and to find solace in the light.

Your story is one of triumph, of rising above the pain and finding purpose. Share your journey, inspire others, and shatter the silence surrounding mental health.

Keep moving forward, even when the road ahead seems uncertain. Draw strength from every step, every breath, and every sunrise. You are a survivor. You are a warrior. You are a beacon of hope.

From the information you have gained from this book, know that you are eventually going to be able to help other people come out of their situation. Subconsciously, you will begin to notice people that are either suicidal or at the verge of losing it. This will be your opportunity to do something worthwhile for yourself and for these people. Just take the step and the universe will carry on and show you other steps to take.

Remember:

You are loved.

You are valued.

You are enough.